Marvelous Symmetry Patterns

COLORING BOOK FOR GROWN UPS
EASY PATTERNS FOR COLORING FUN

by Kelly Dombrowski

Marvelous Symmetry Patterns
Coloring Book for Grown Ups

Easy Patterns for Coloring Fun

Copyright © 2016 by Kelly Dombrowski
www.coloringbooknut.com

ISBN-13: 978-1532895555

ISBN-10: 1532895550

Printed in U.S.A

How to Use This Book

If you choose to use markers or any medium that will bleed through to the other side, copy and print on card stock. You have permission to reproduce the pages for your personal use. You can try coloring them several different ways!

Most of all, have fun. If the spaces are too small, leave them white. If you need to do something, touch them up with a black fine tip marker. Don't fuss over how to fill those spaces!

Relax and have your favorite drink or snack nearby. Put on some music or listen to your favorite TV show and color! Enjoy the process!

Never mind those lines. If you go over them, no one cares, you are enjoying yourself! And sometimes it's good therapy just to color with any old color that you fancy at the time! You don't need to show any of your work to anyone.

If you wish to improve, over time you will get better! Everyone can learn how to color like a professional with practice.

My hope is that this will be a gateway to more creative endeavors! Maybe someday you will try drawing your coloring pages or pick up a paint brush and start painting!

Visit *www.ColoringBookNut.com* for color ideas tips and tricks!

Have Fun!!

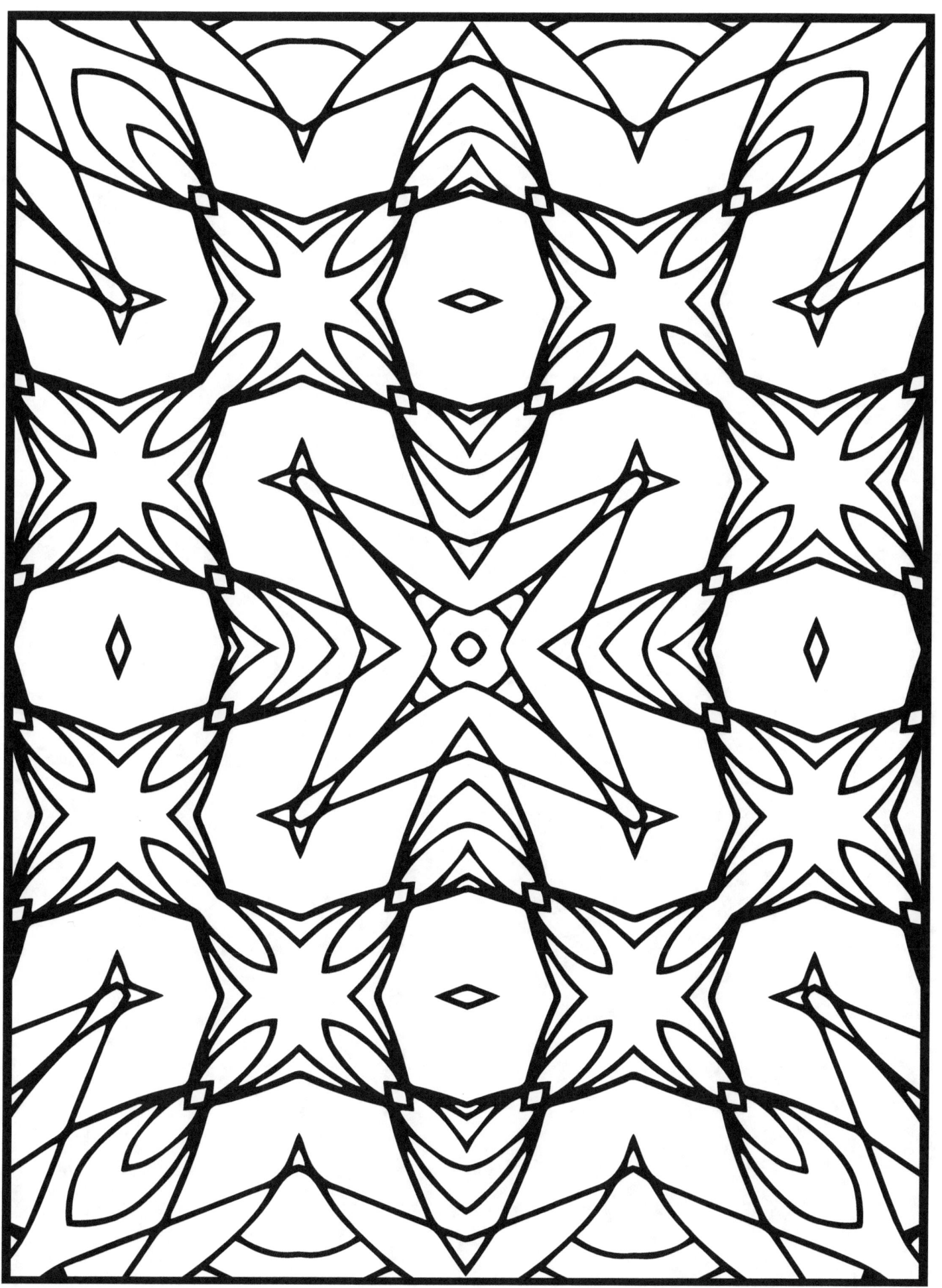

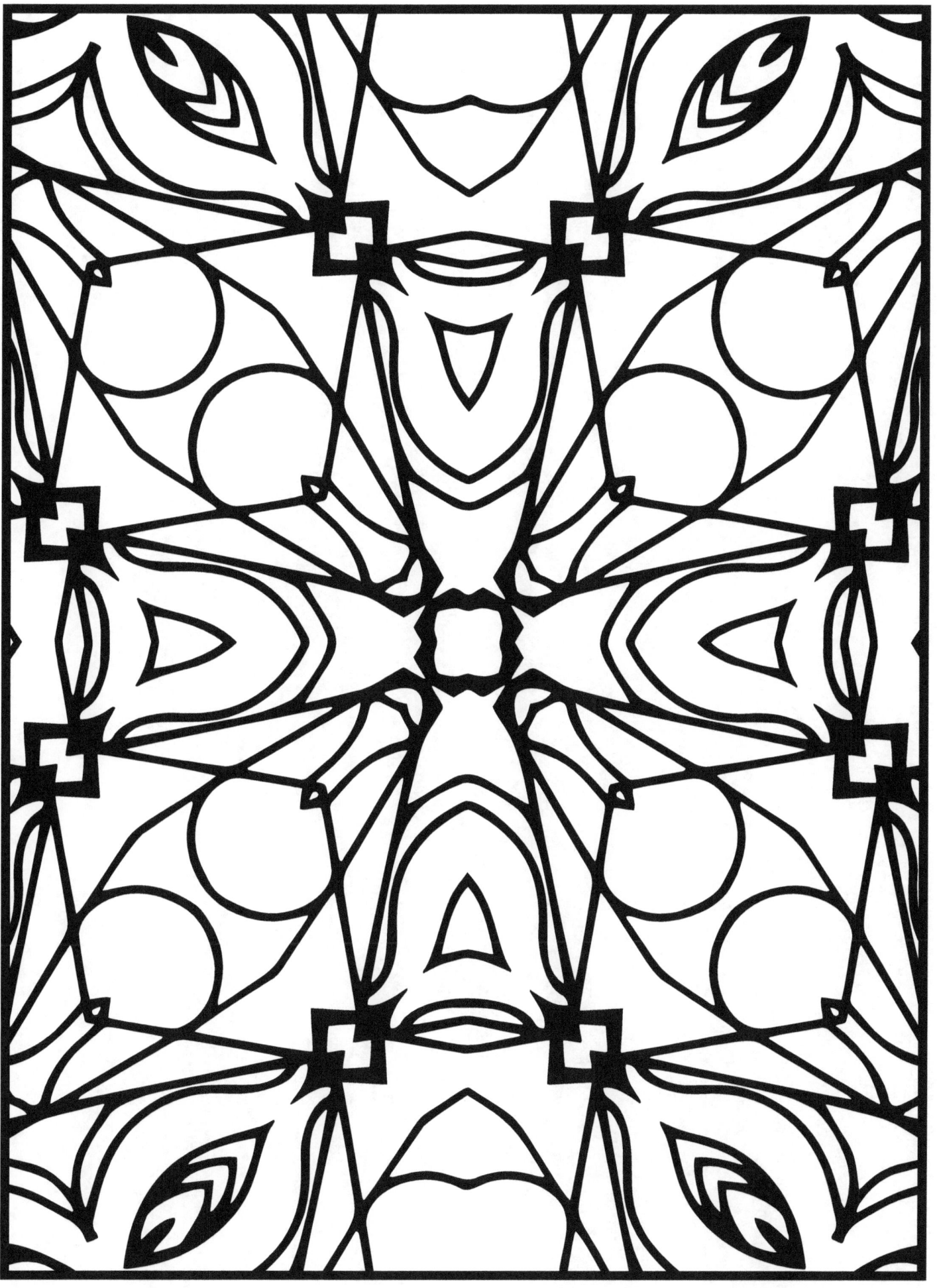

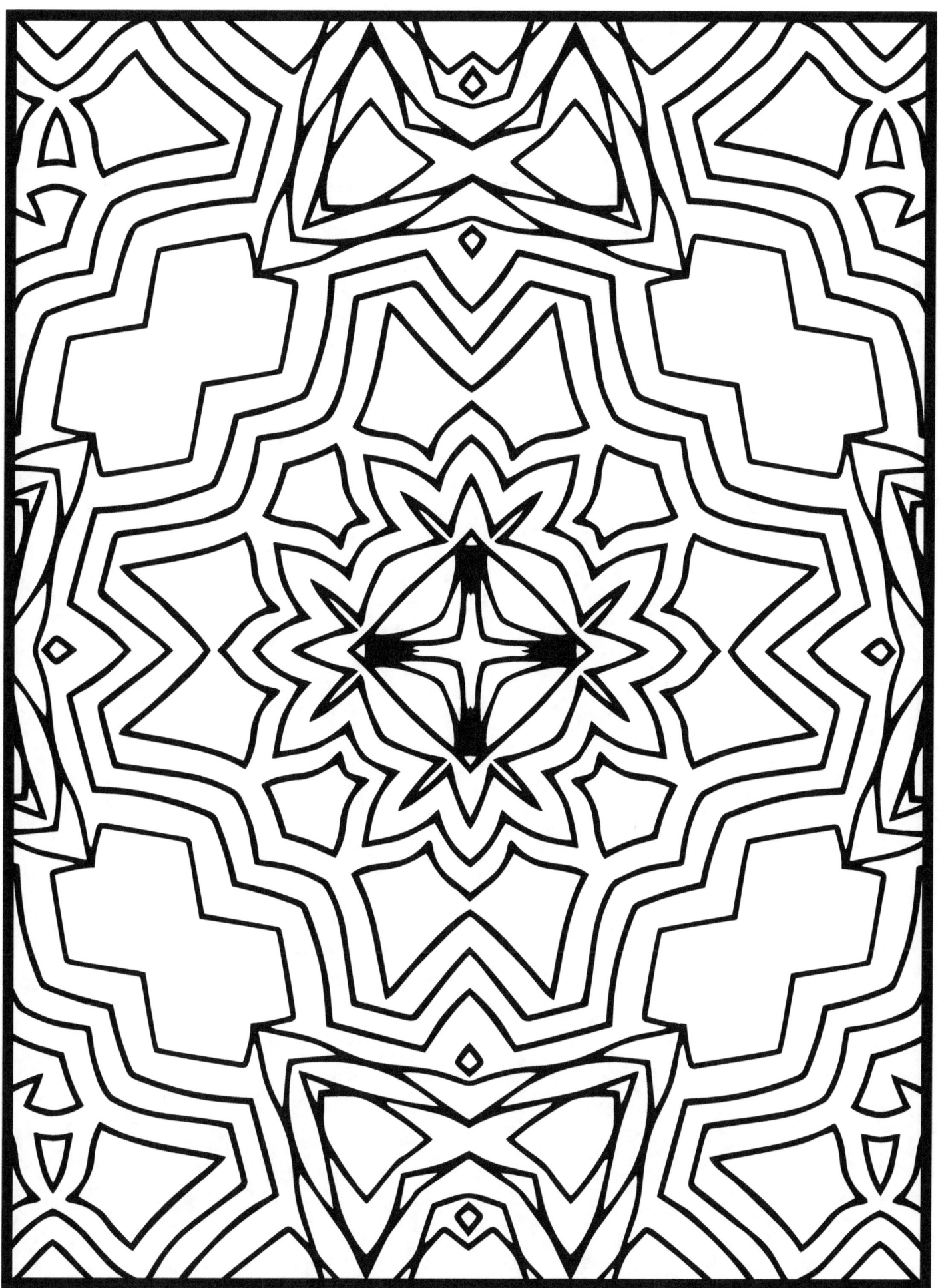

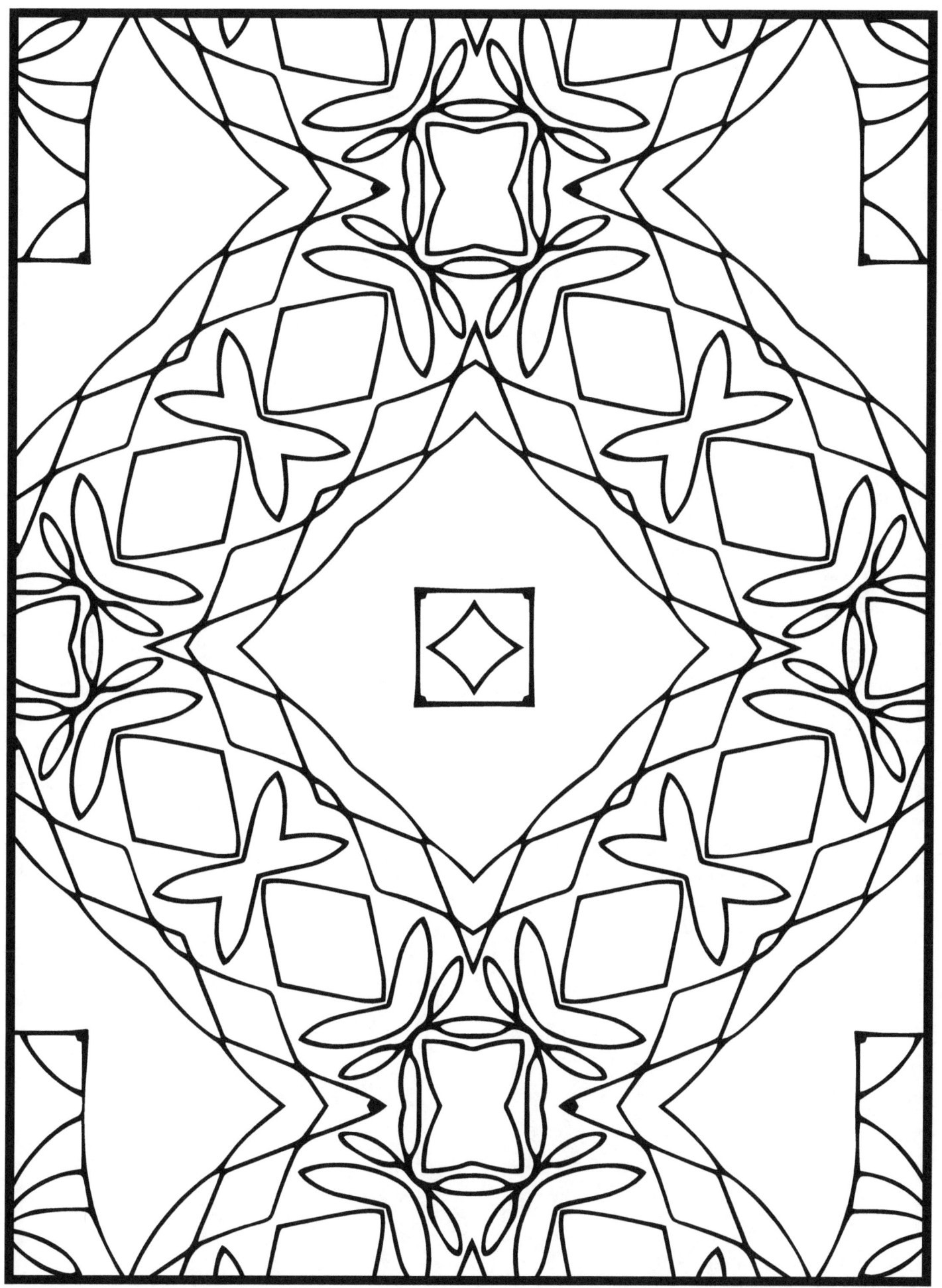

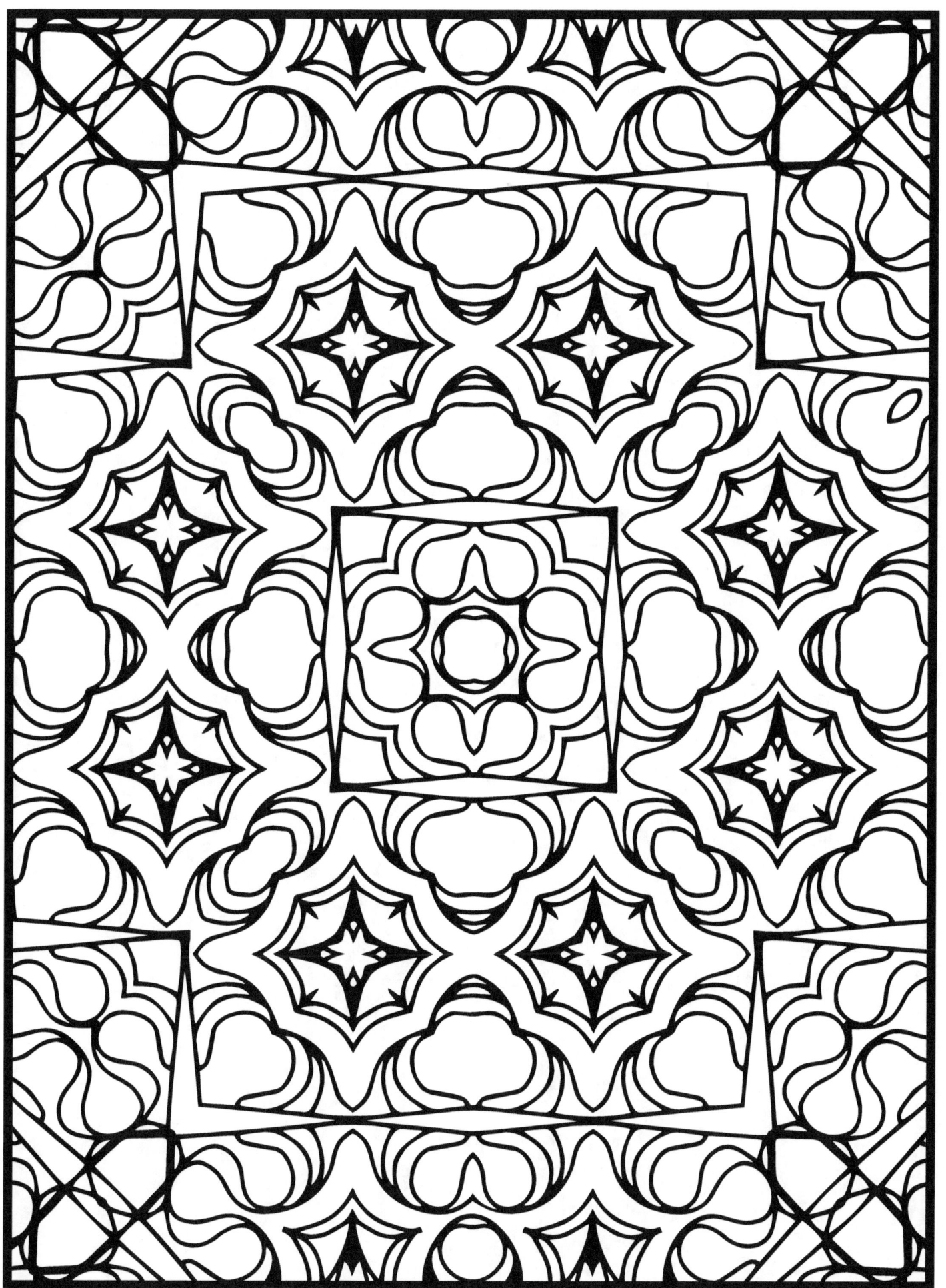

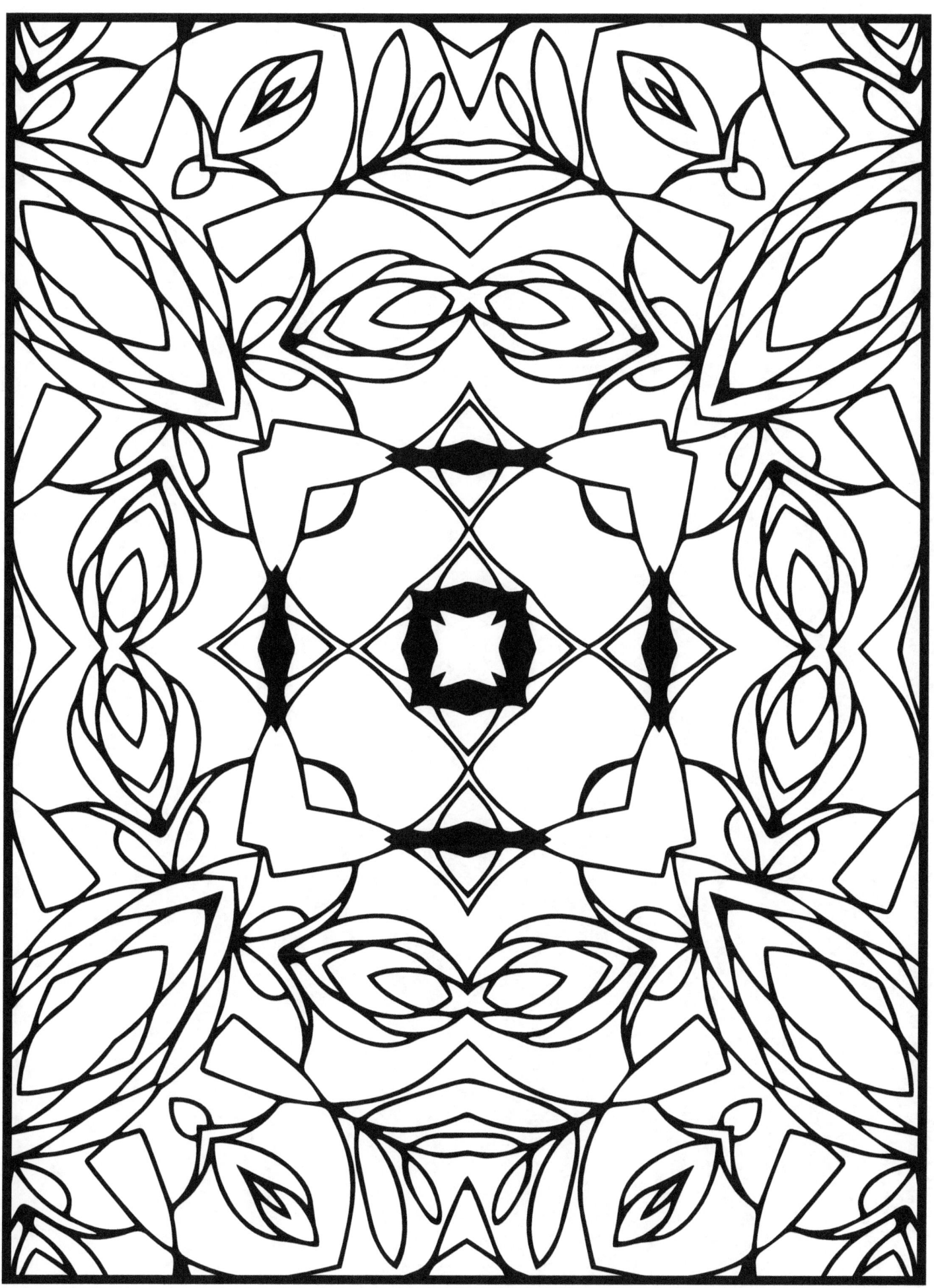

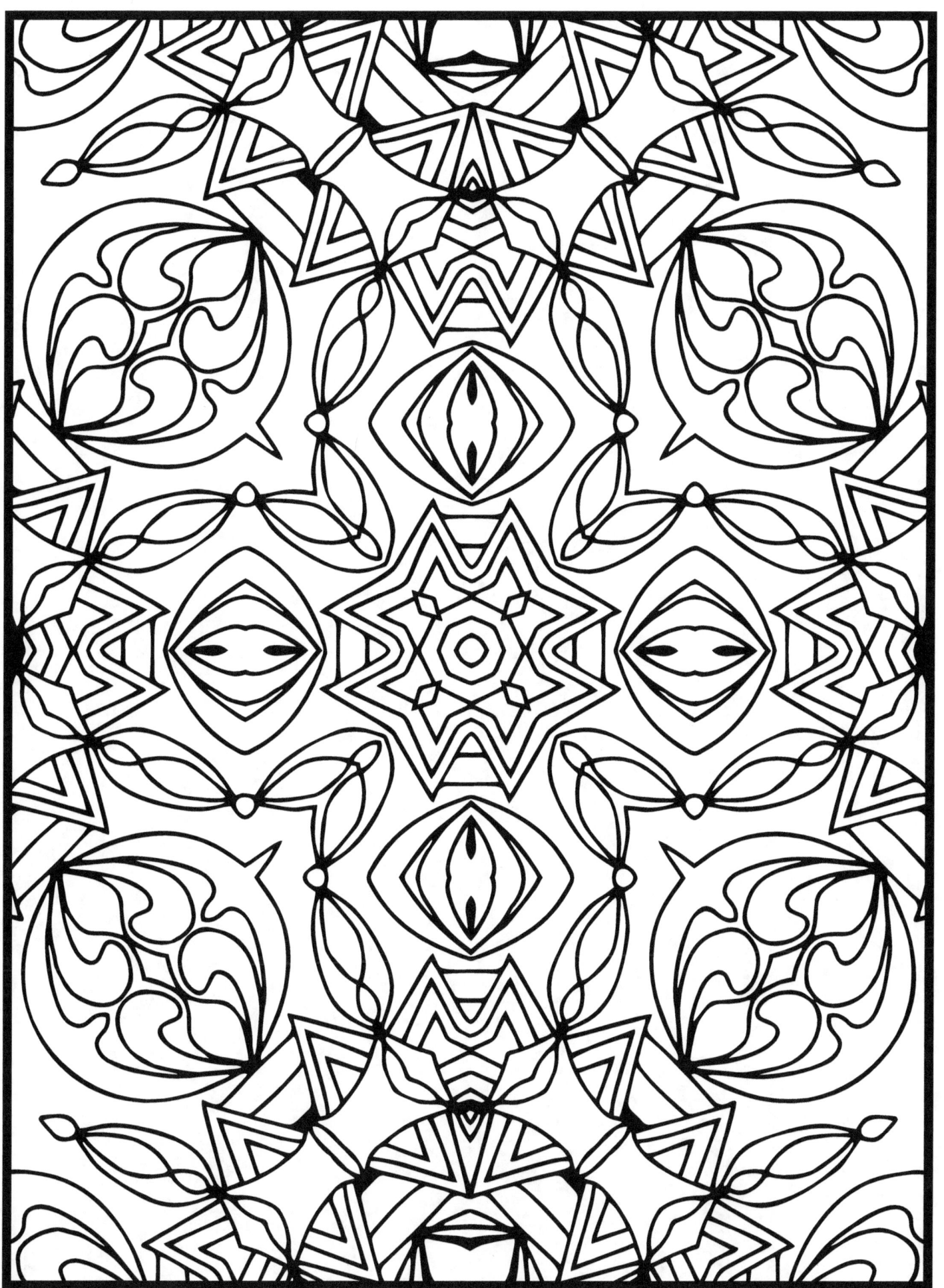

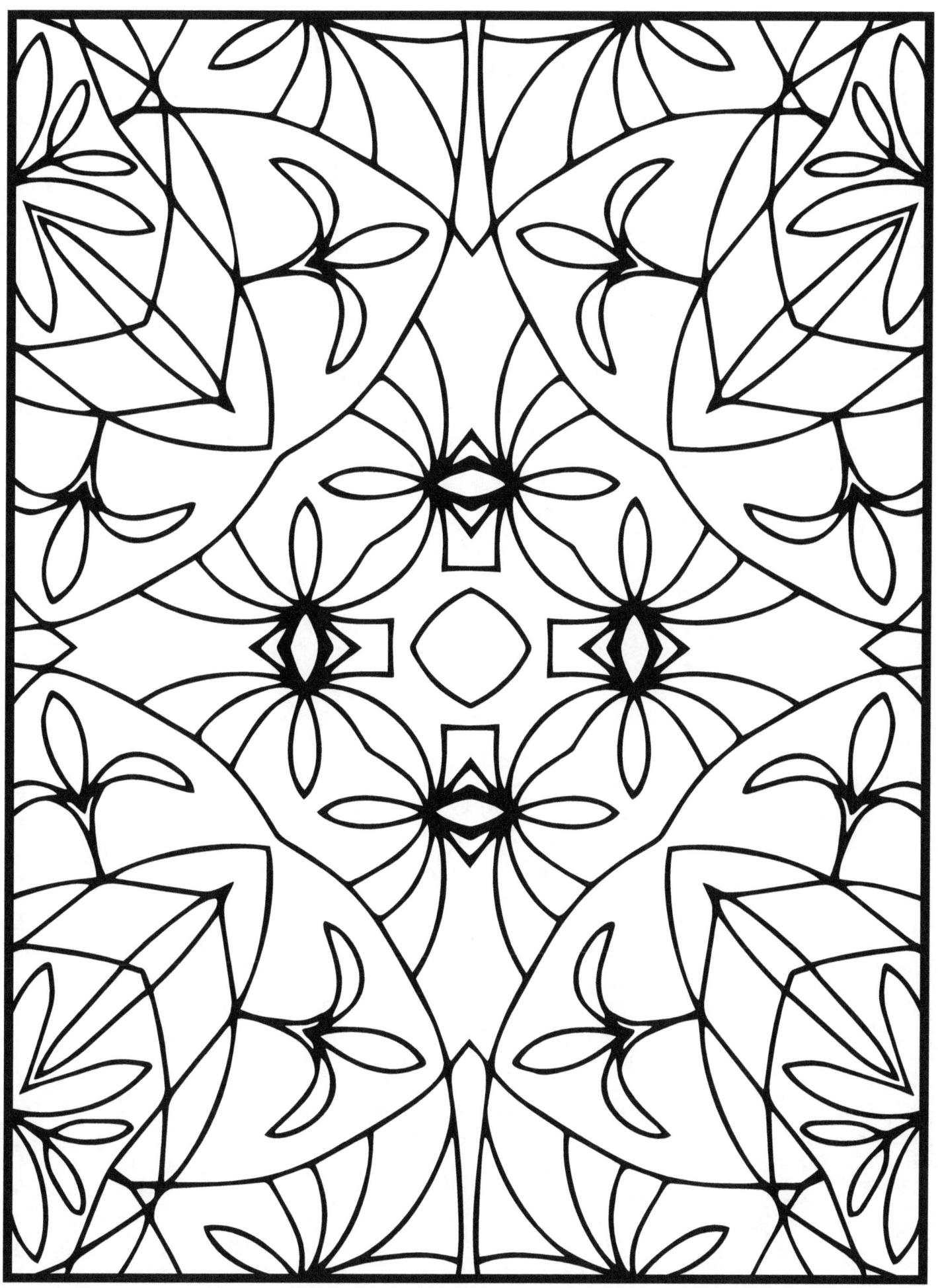

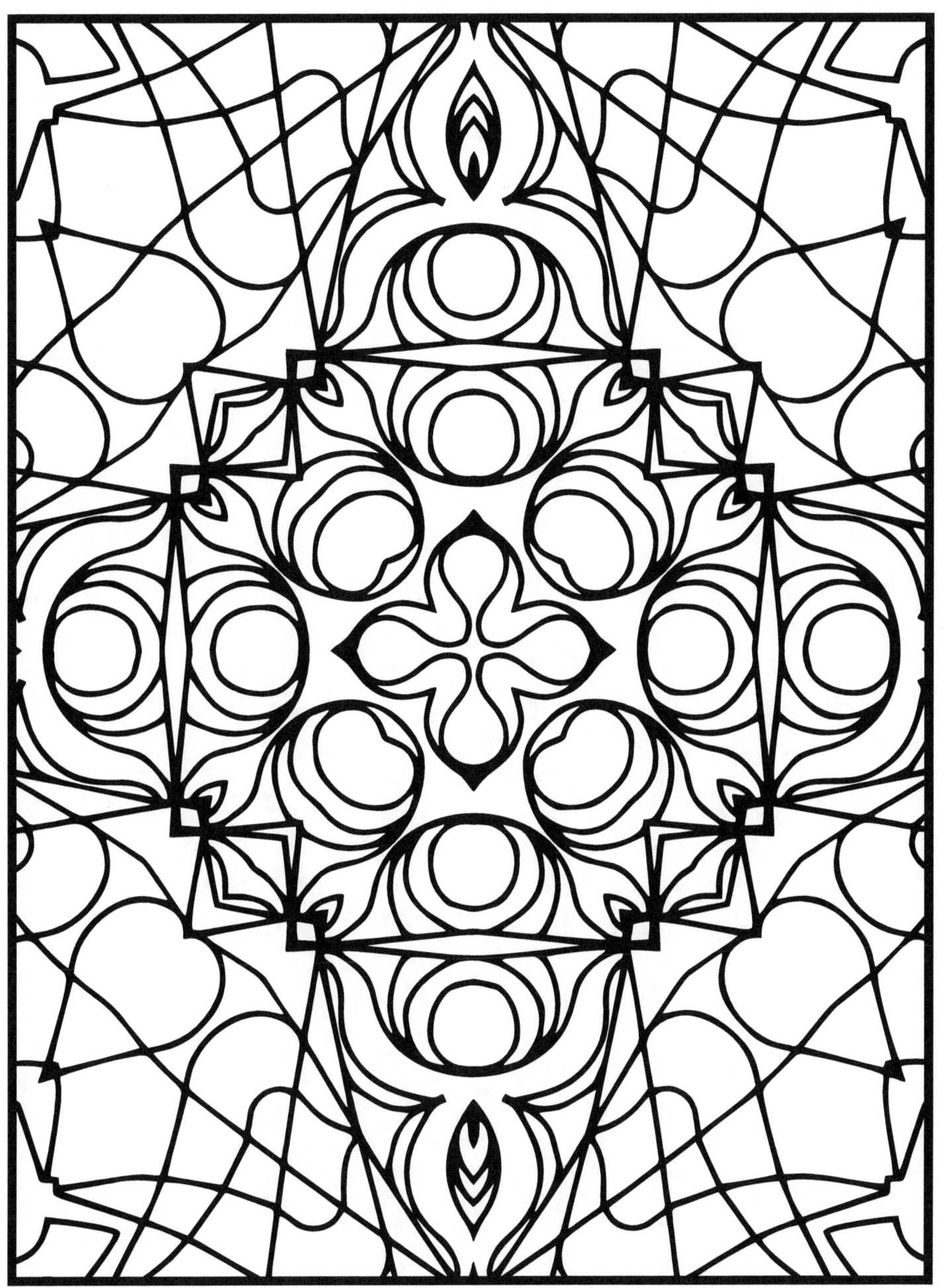

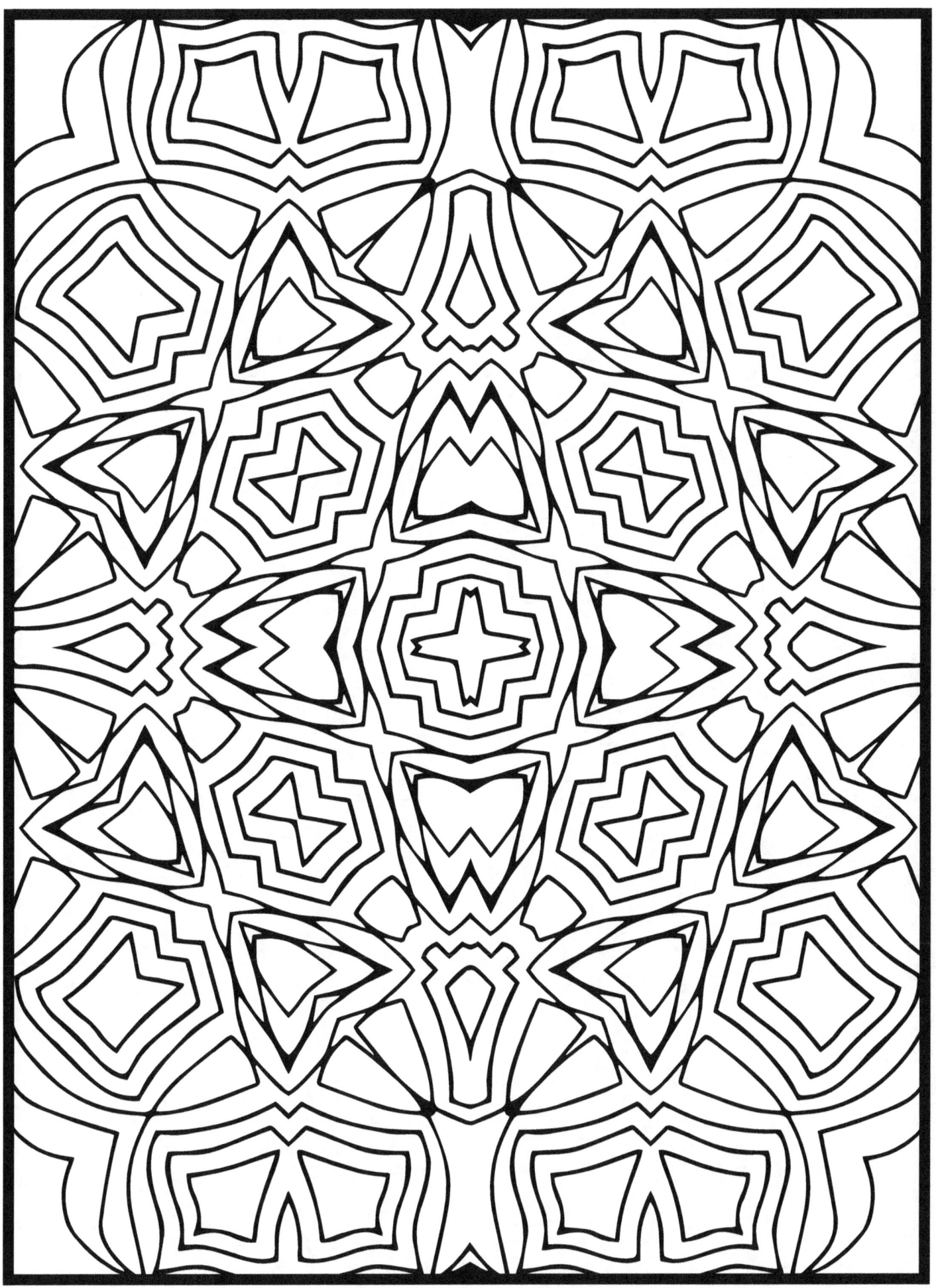

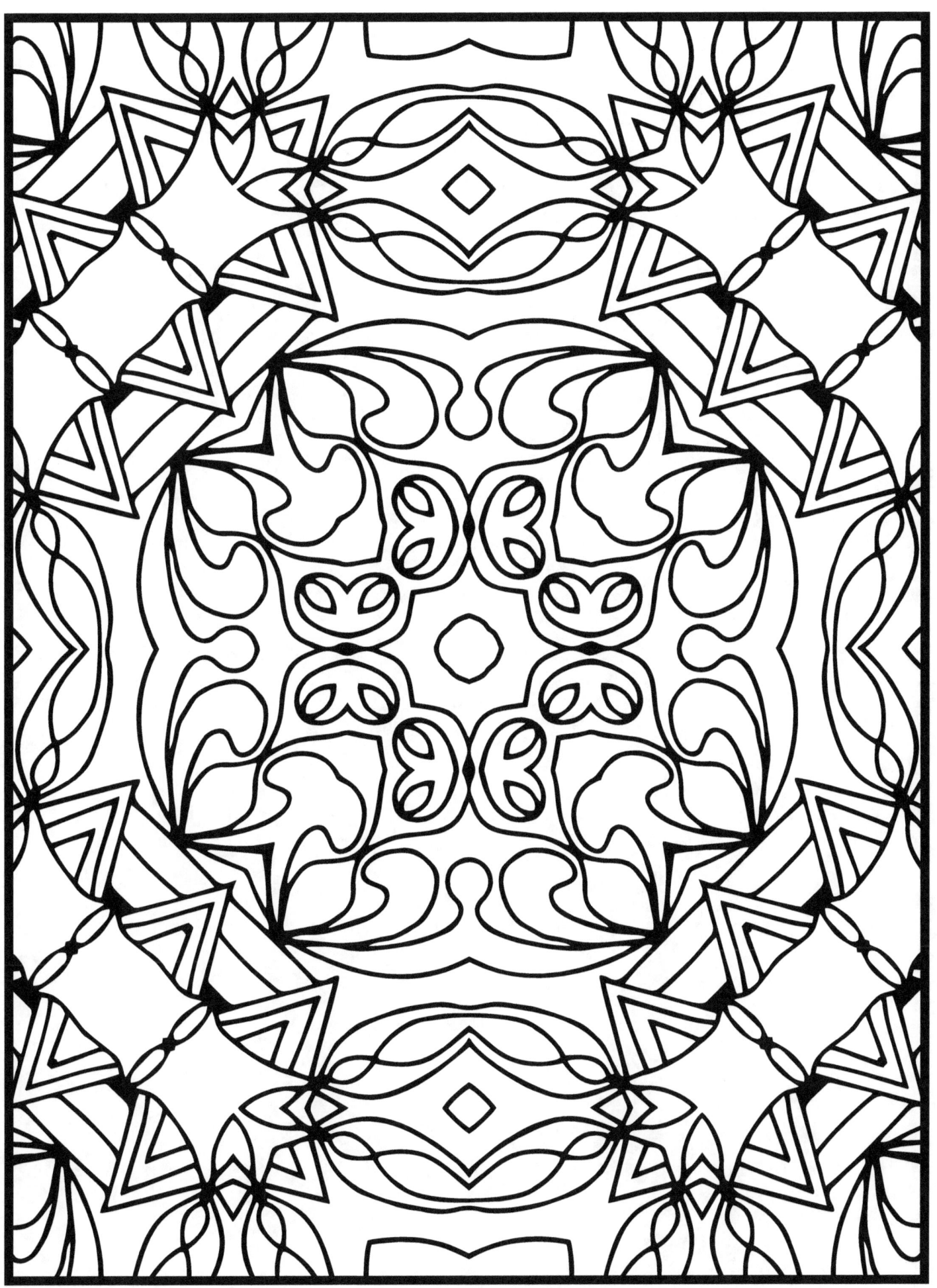

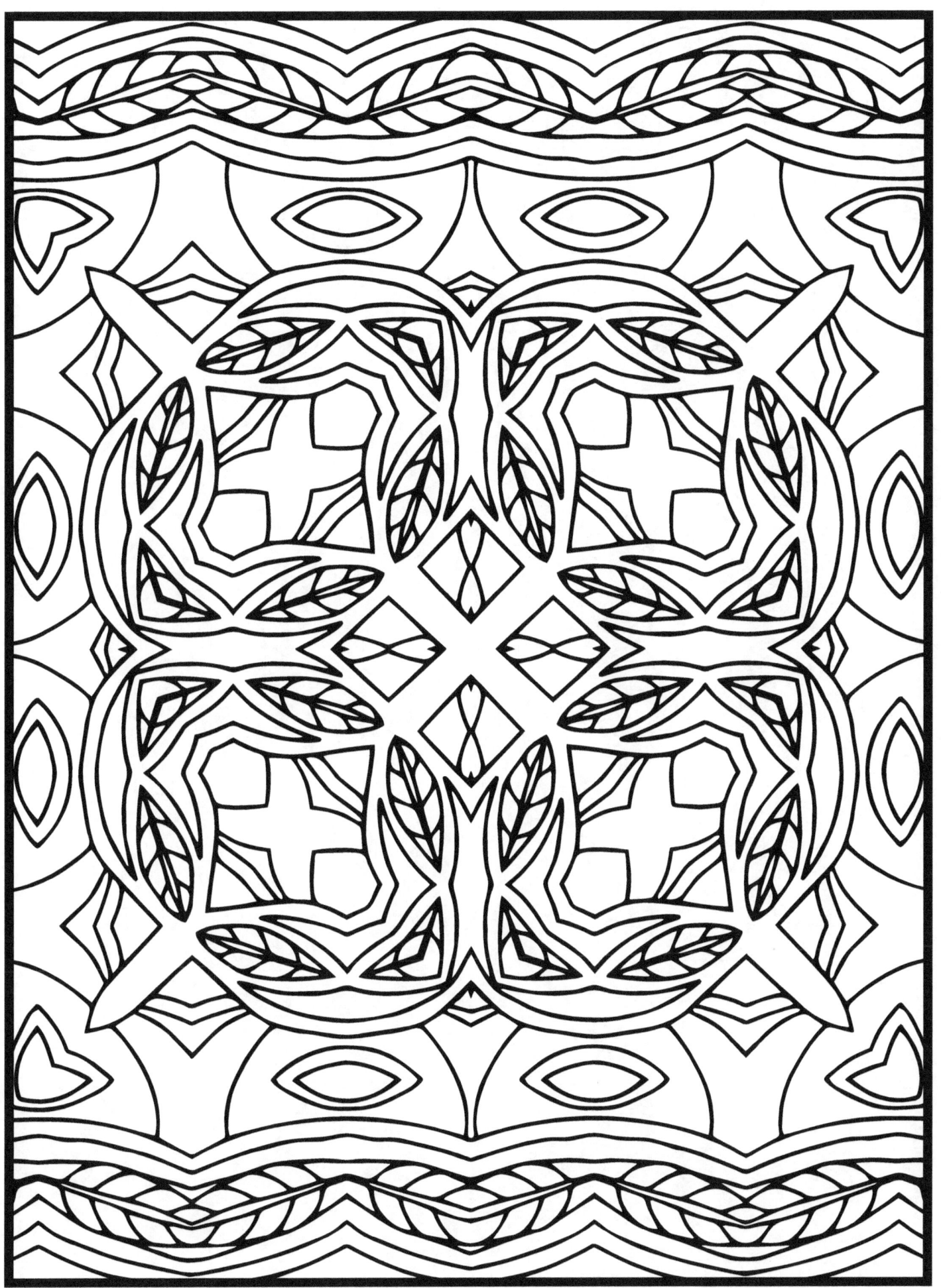

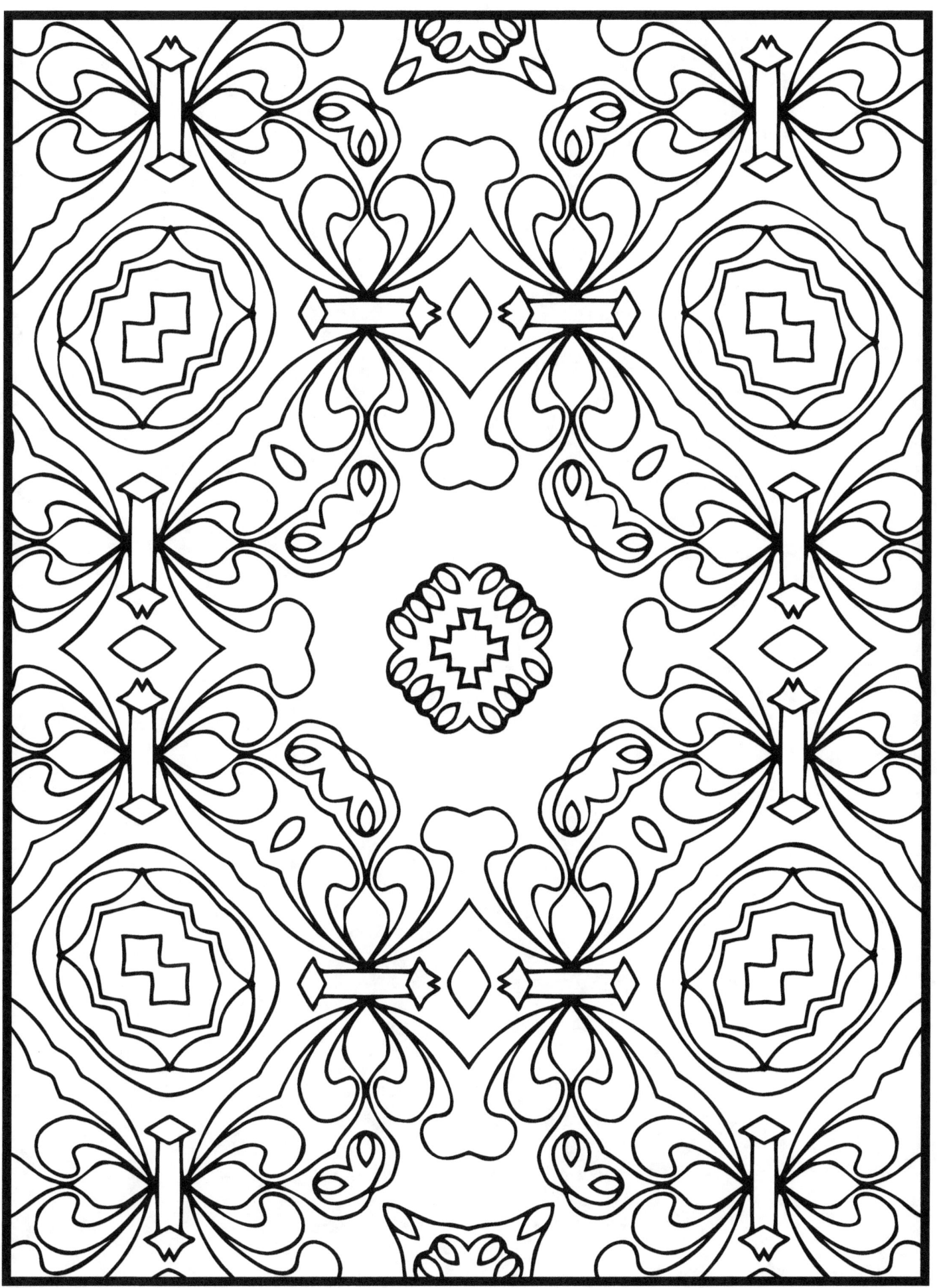

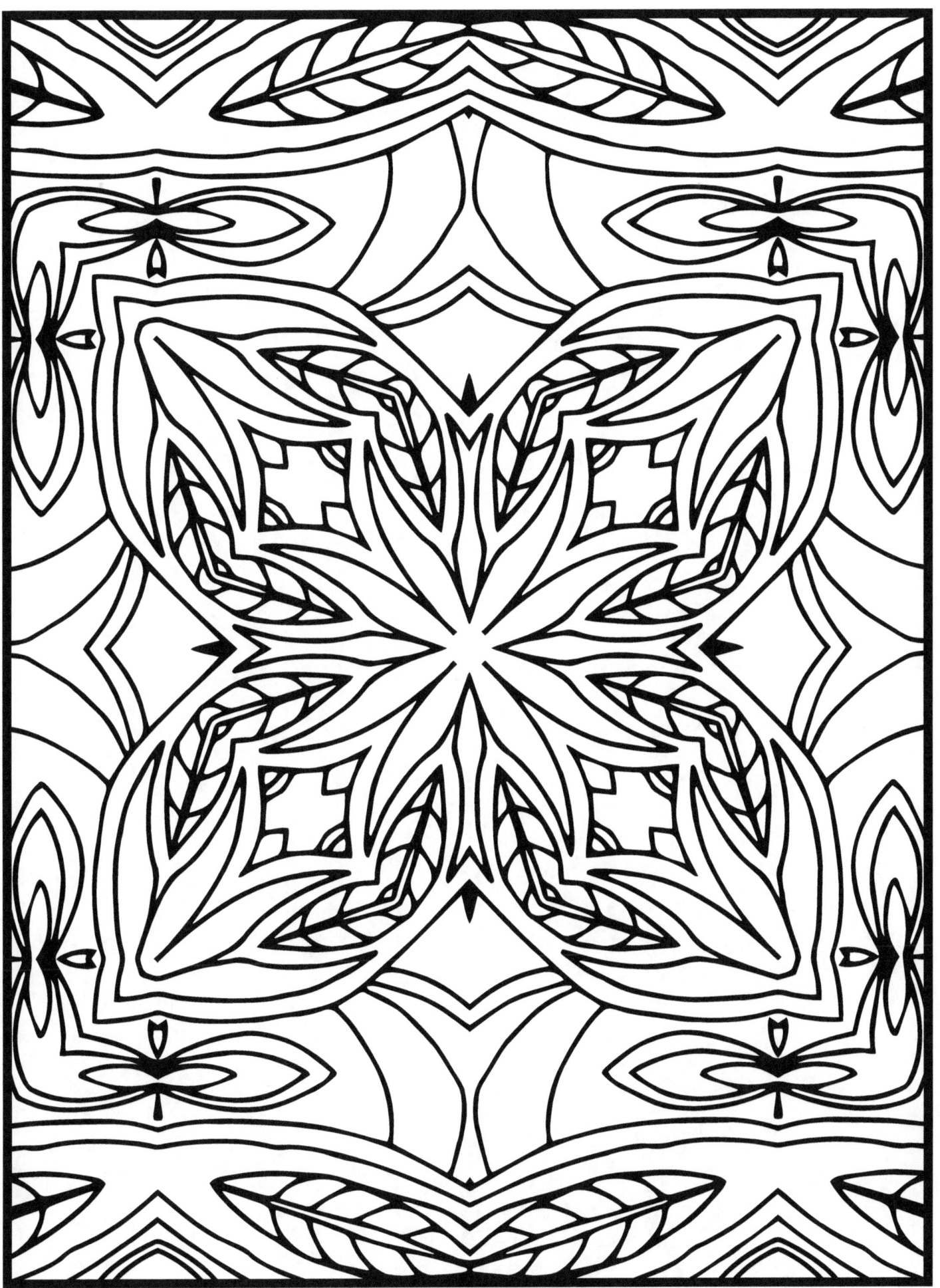

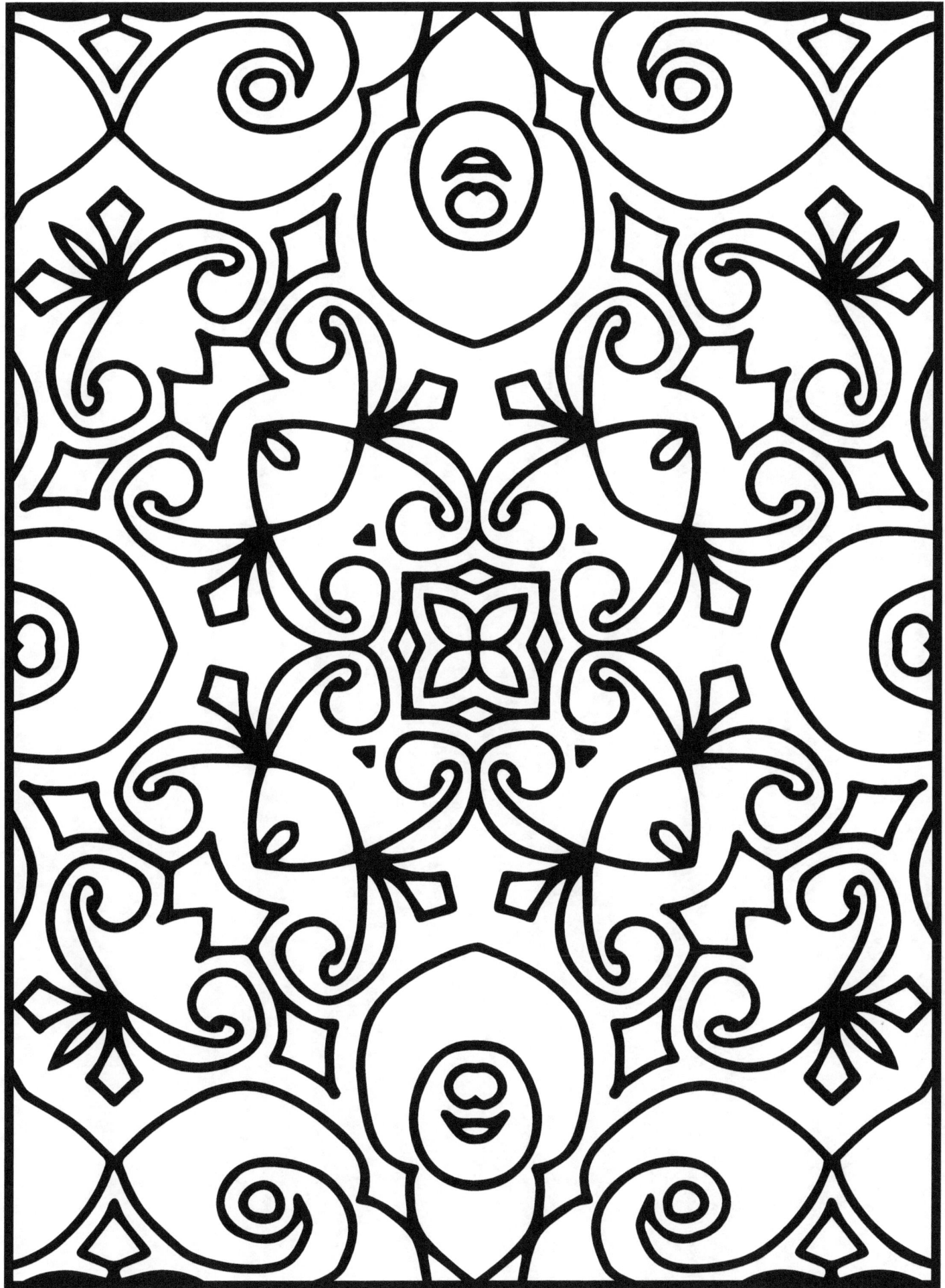

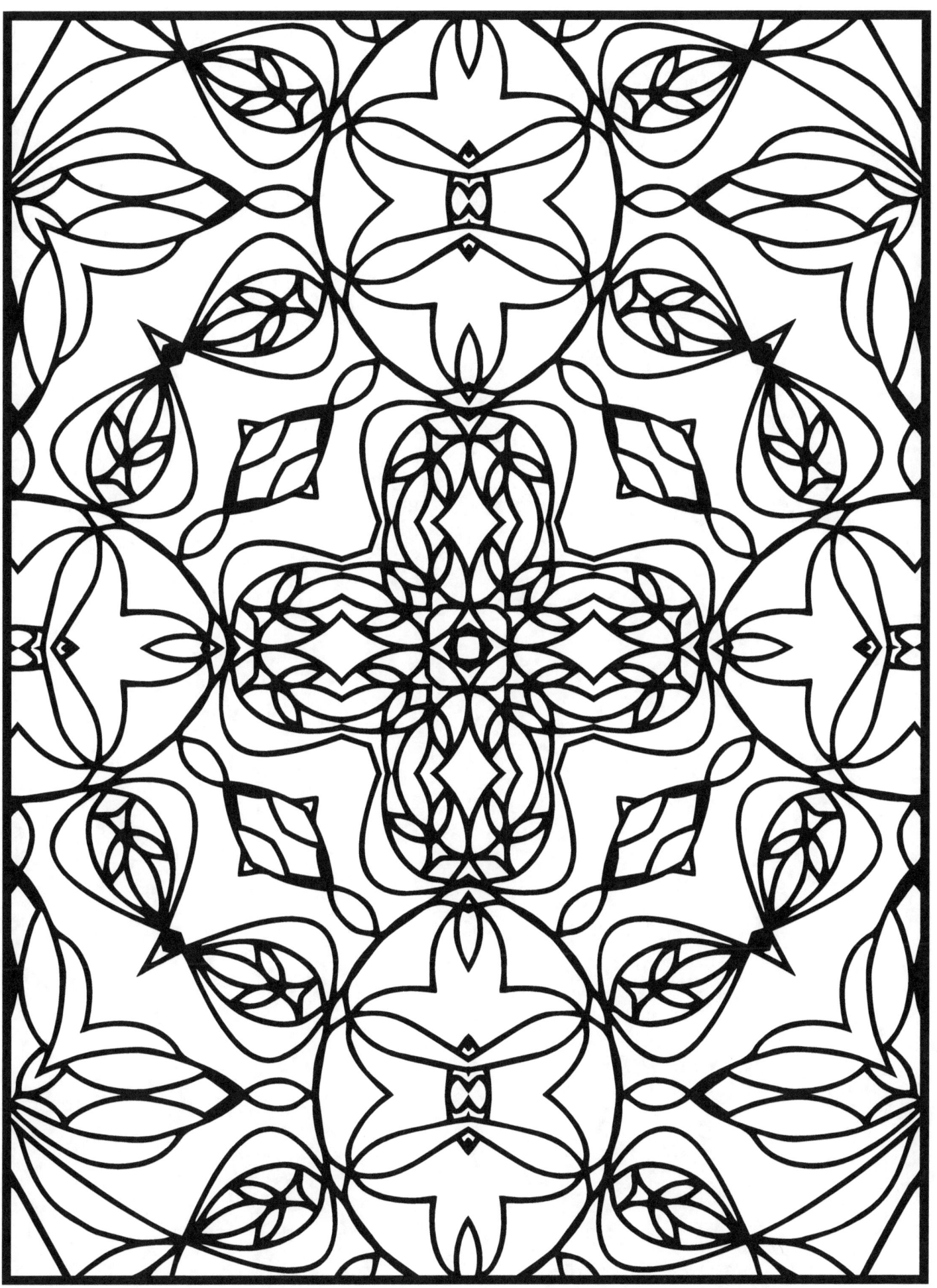

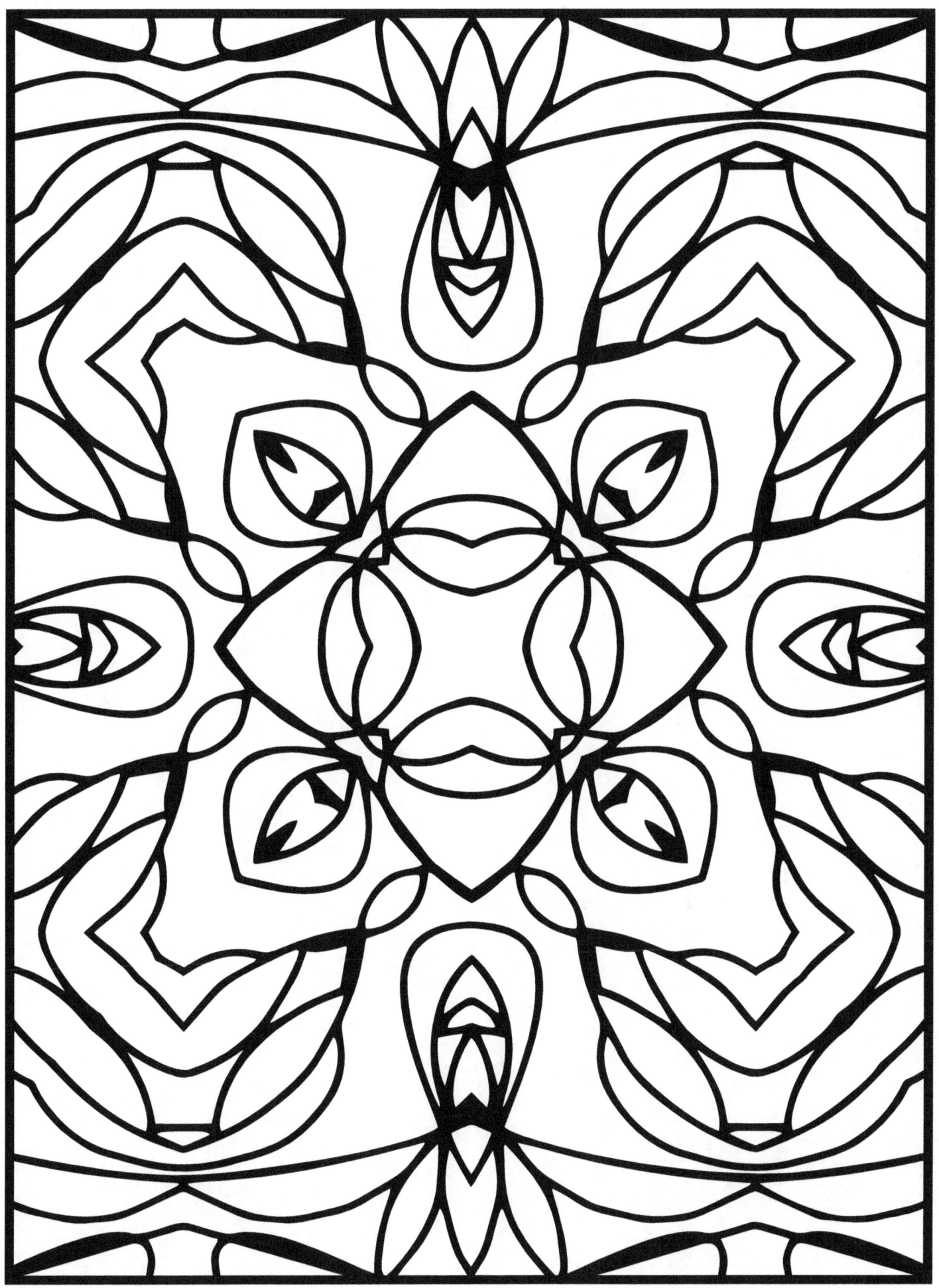

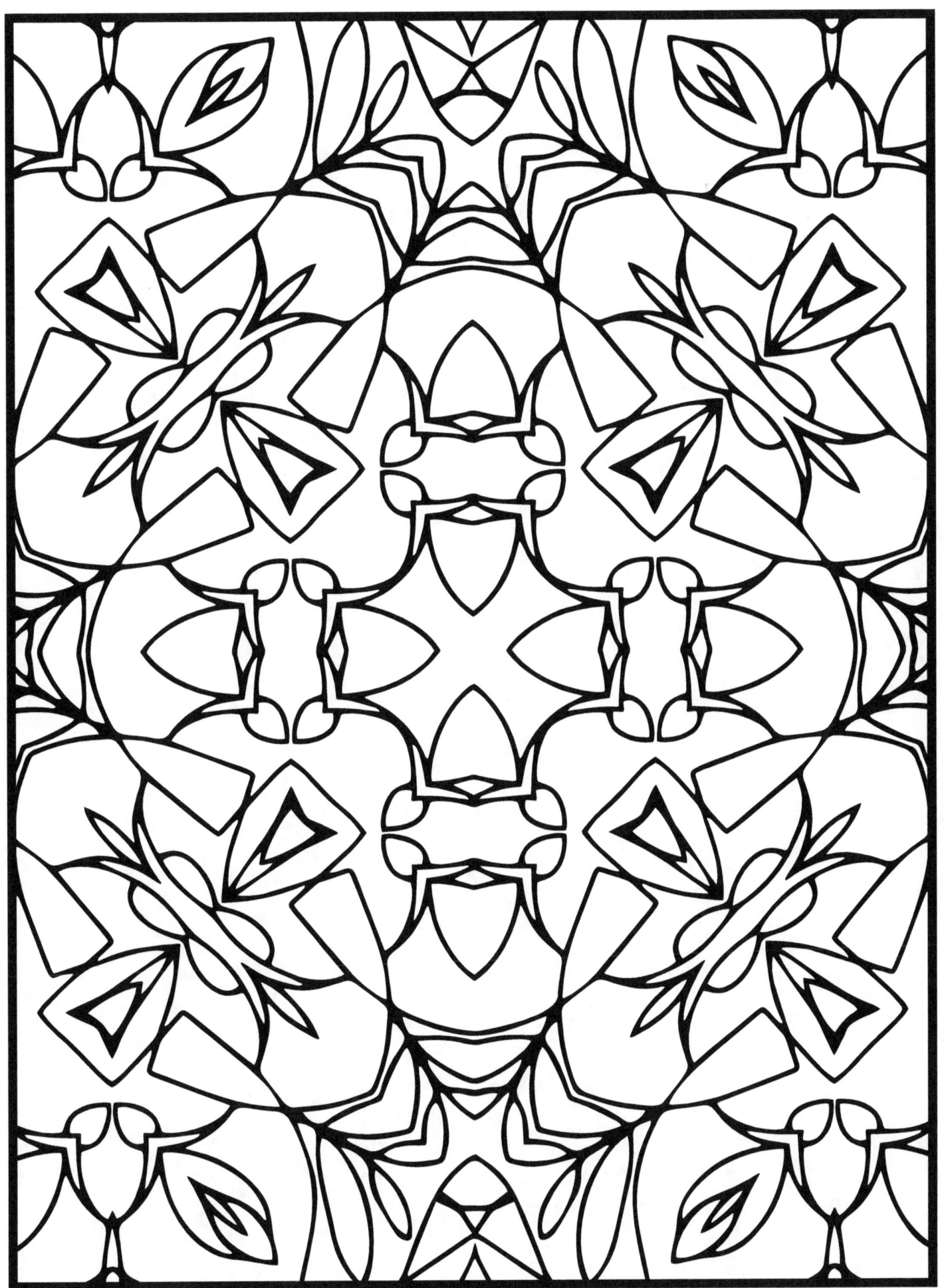

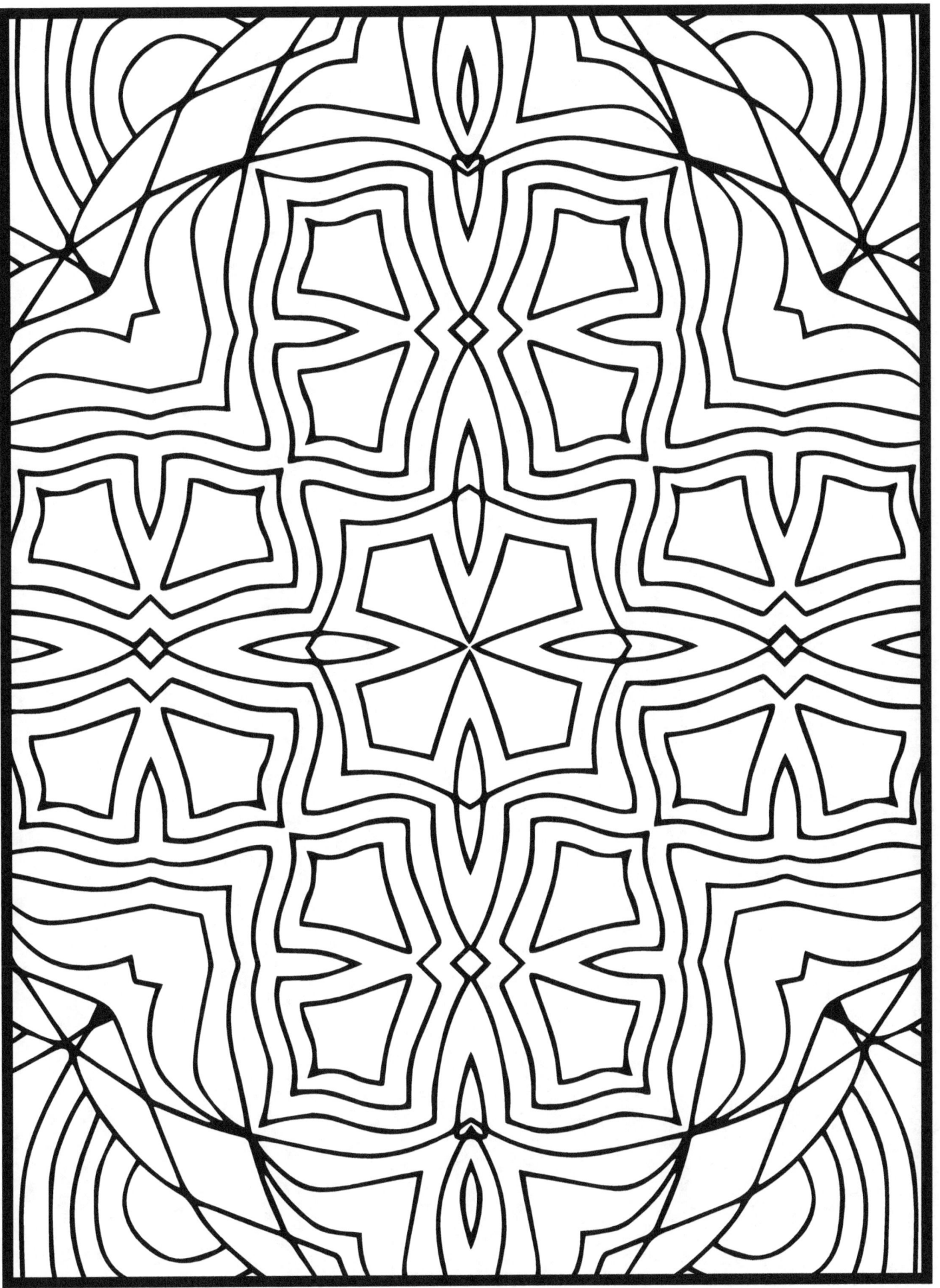

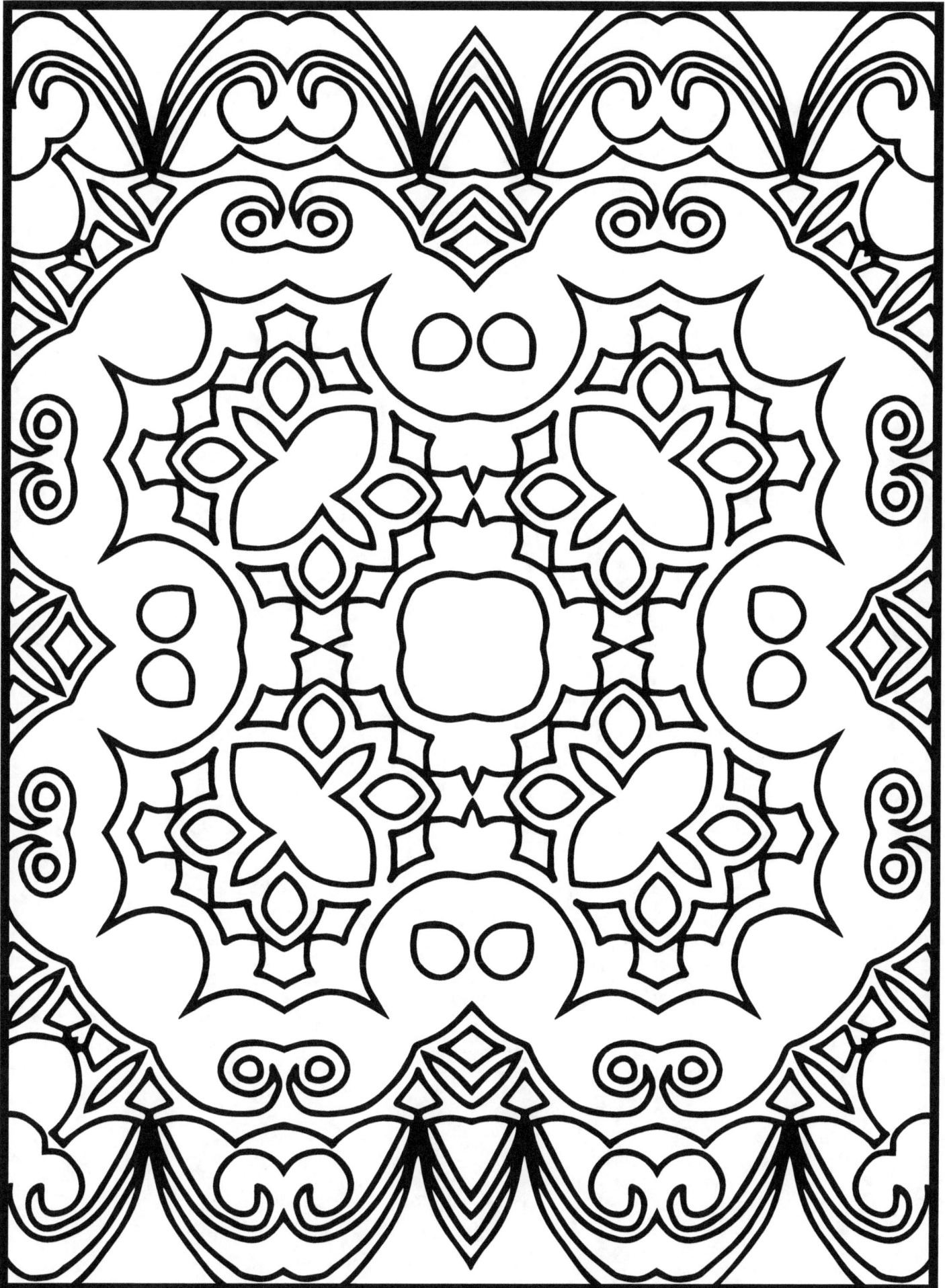

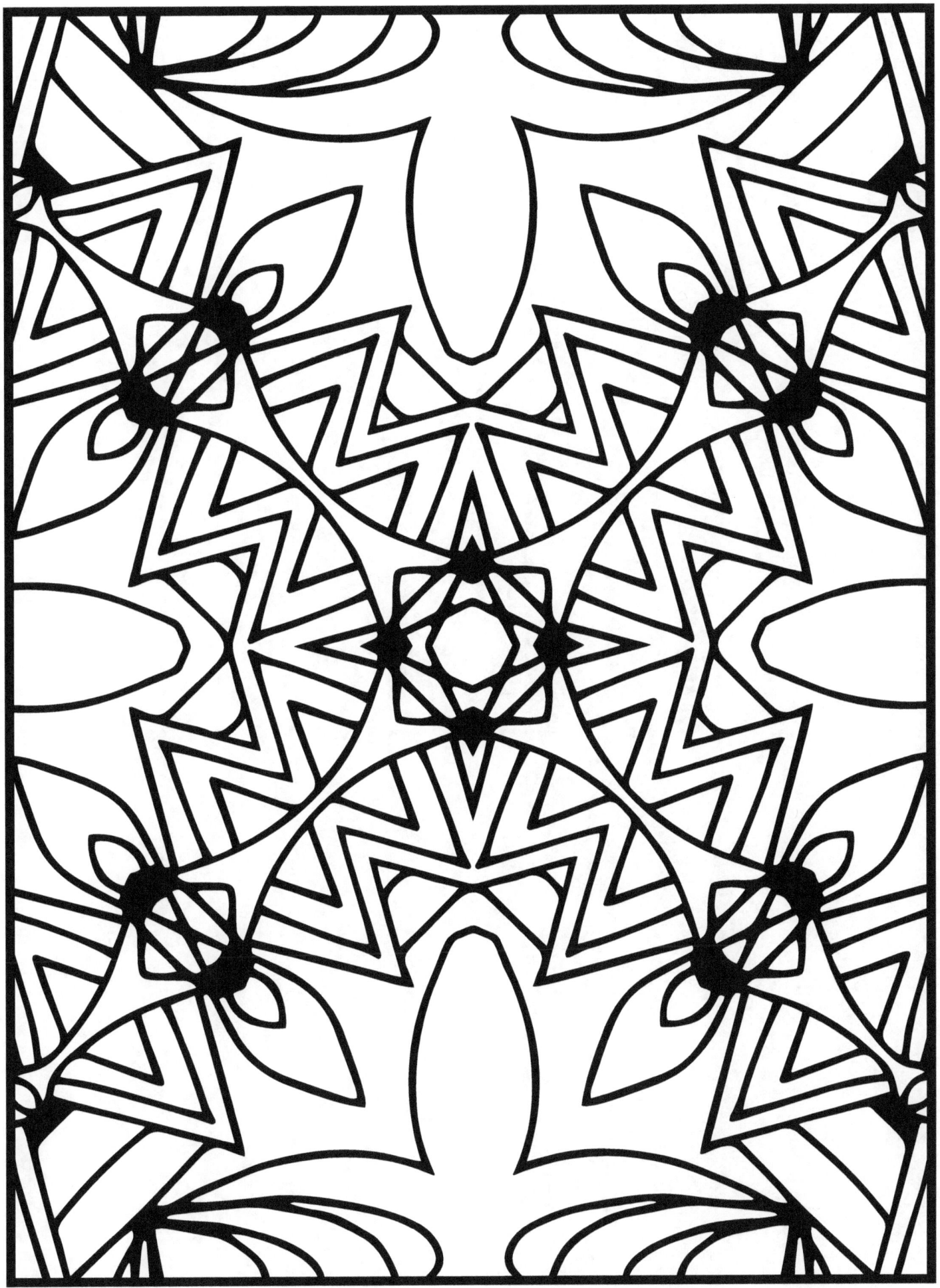

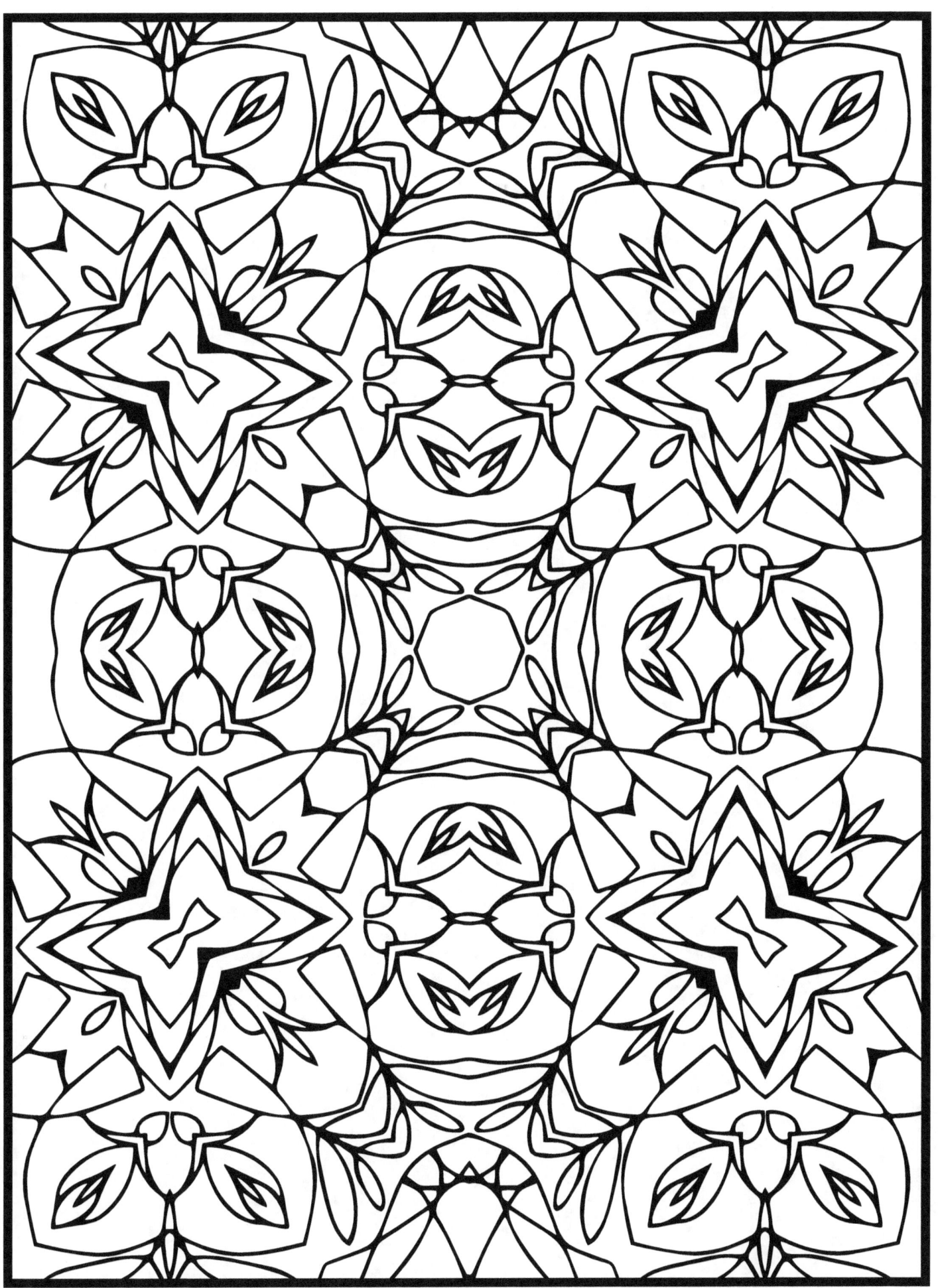

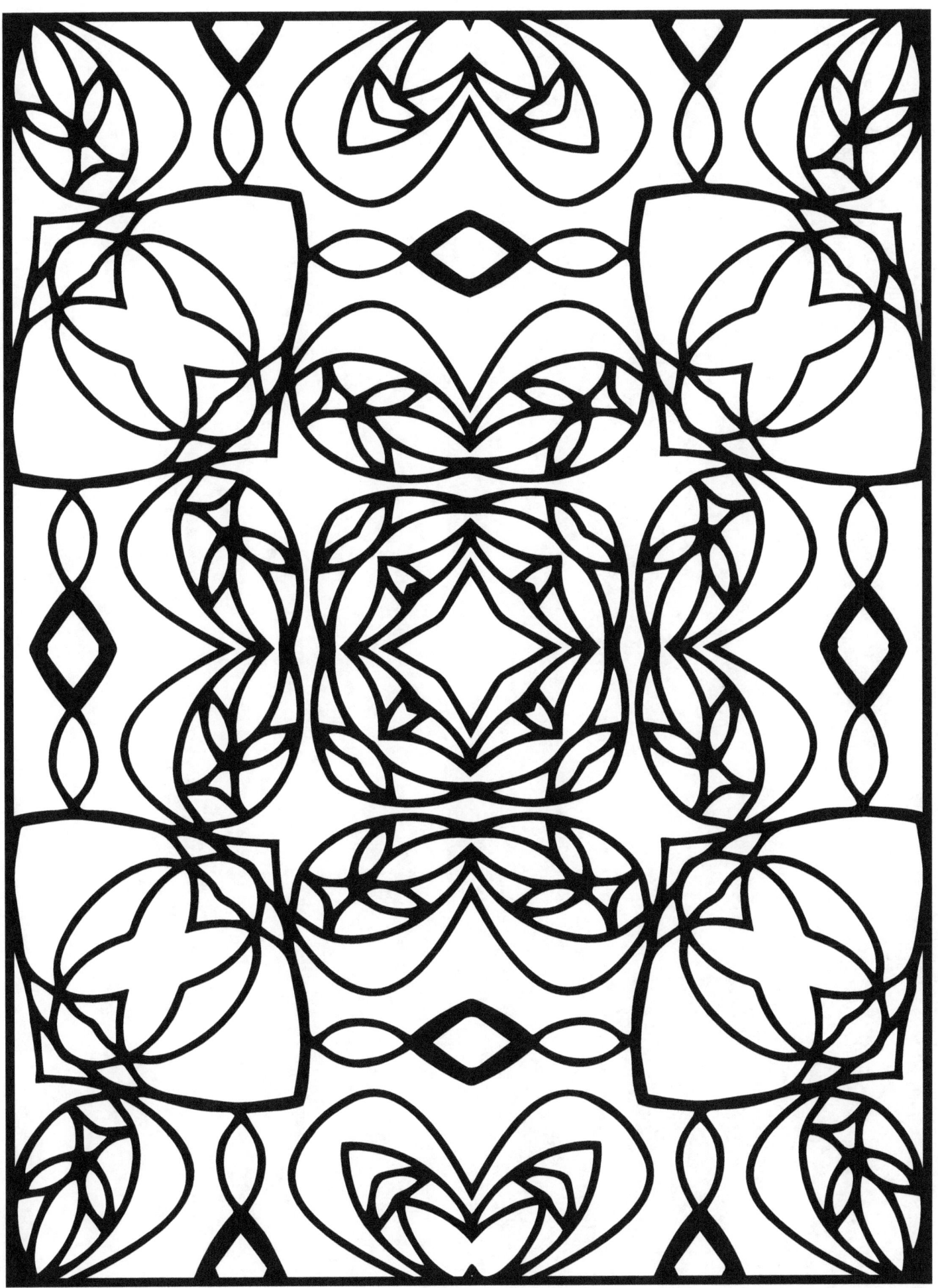

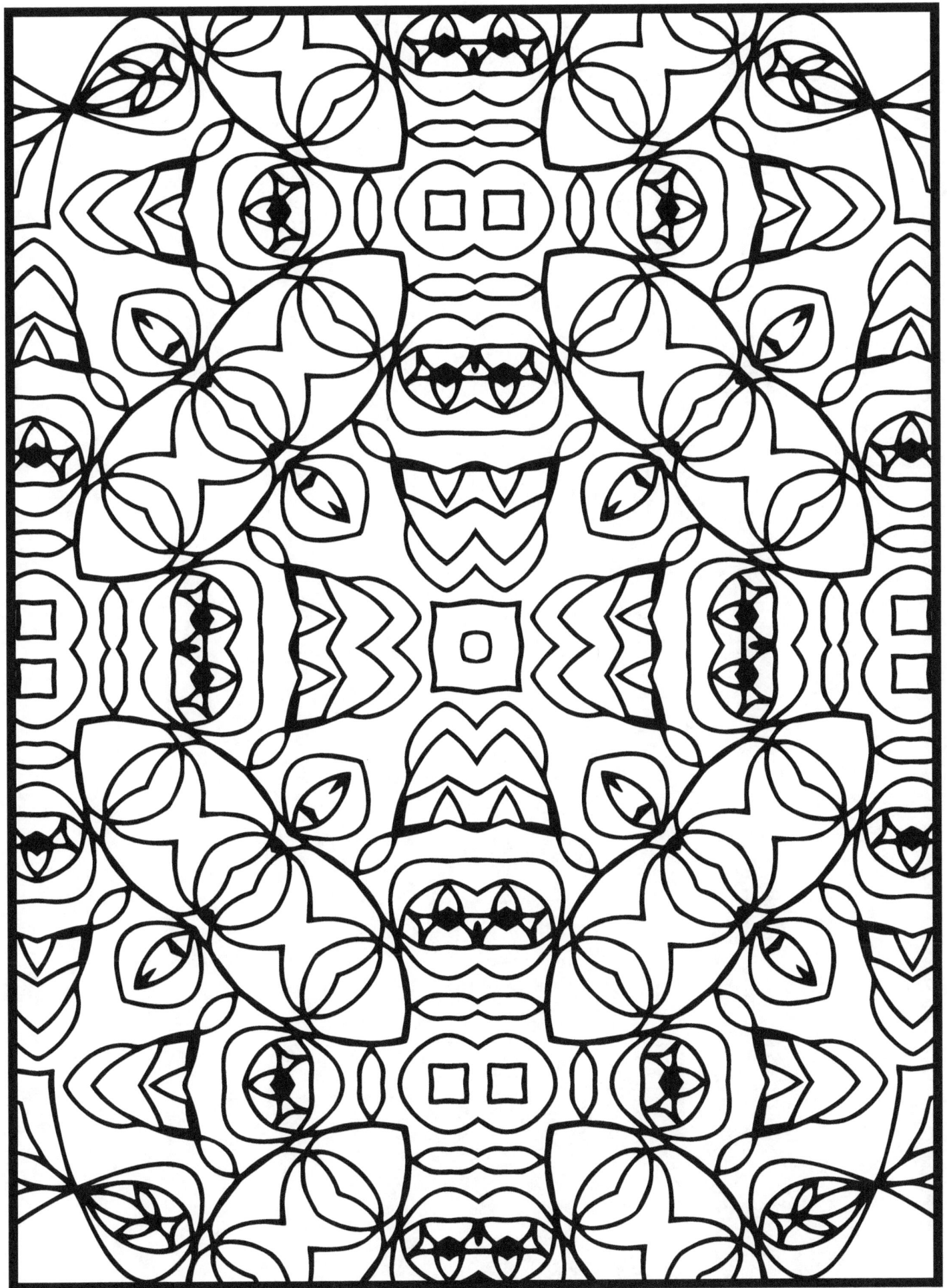

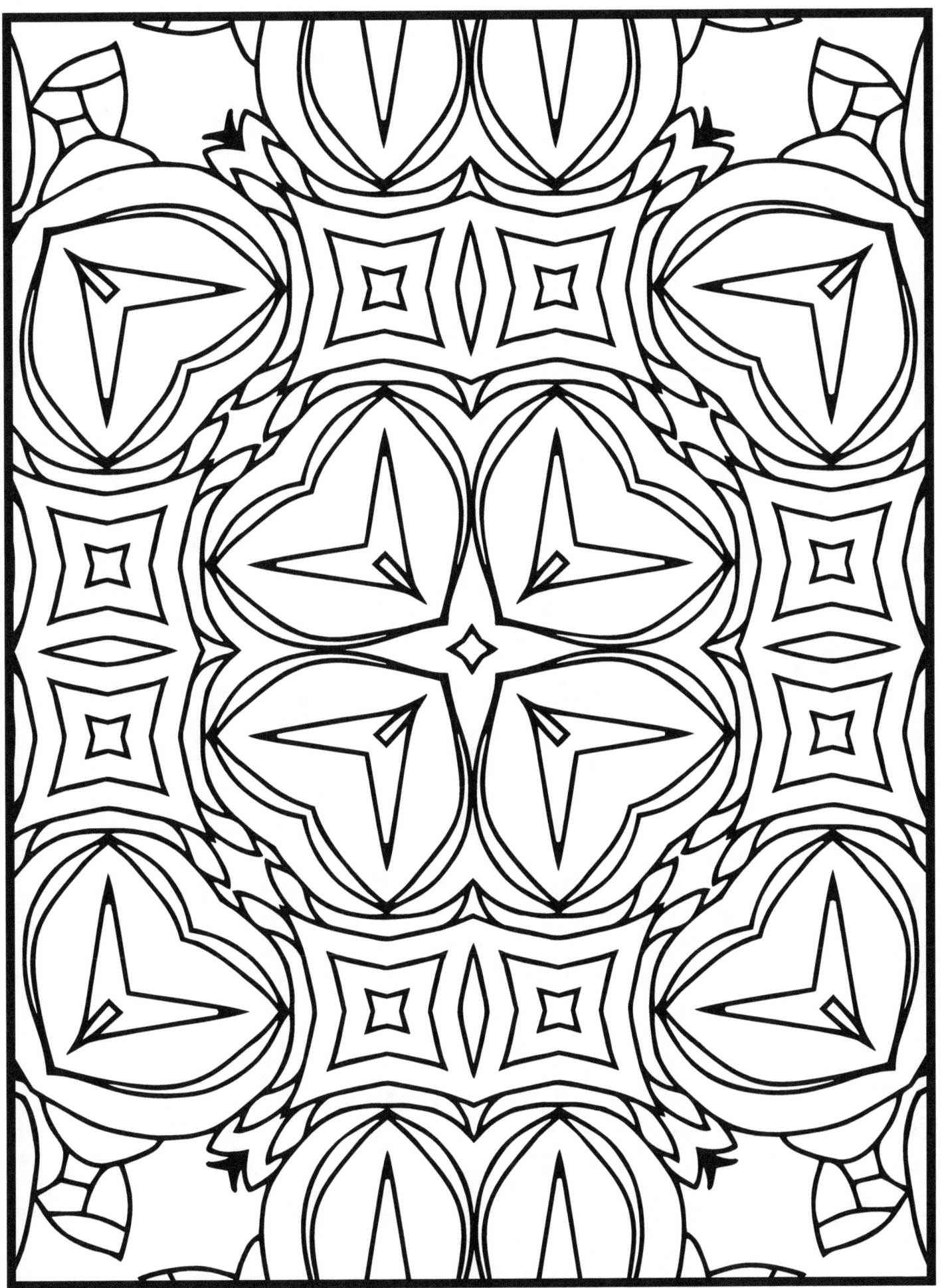

Visit us on social media!

Show us what you have done
and let us share your awesome coloring skills!

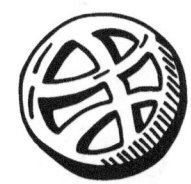 www.ColoringBookNut.com

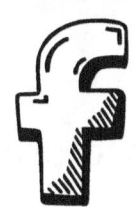 The Coloring Book Nut

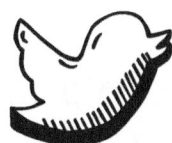 @KellytheArtist

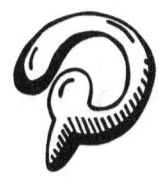 Kelly Dombrowski

 KellyDombrowskiArt

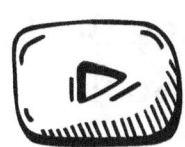 The Coloring Book Nut

Look for these and other books by Kelly Dombrowski on Amazon.com

Kaleidoscopes Unleashed: An Adventure in Adult Coloring
Beginner Volume 1

Kaleidoscopes Unleashed: An Adventure in Adult Coloring
Intermediate Volume 1

Kaleidoscopes Unleashed: An Adventure in Adult Coloring
Advanced Volume 1

Sweet Curly Cue Designs: An Adventure in Adult Coloring
Volume 1

Sweet Curly Cue Designs: An Adventure in Adult Coloring
Volume 2

Powerful Positive Affirmations Adult Coloring Book:
Coloring for Health, Happiness and Wholeness

Inspirational Positive Affirmations Adult Coloring Book:
Nurturing and Loving Words to Feed Your Soul

Daylight and Midnight Symmetry Patterns: Quick Easy Fun Coloring
For Grown Ups

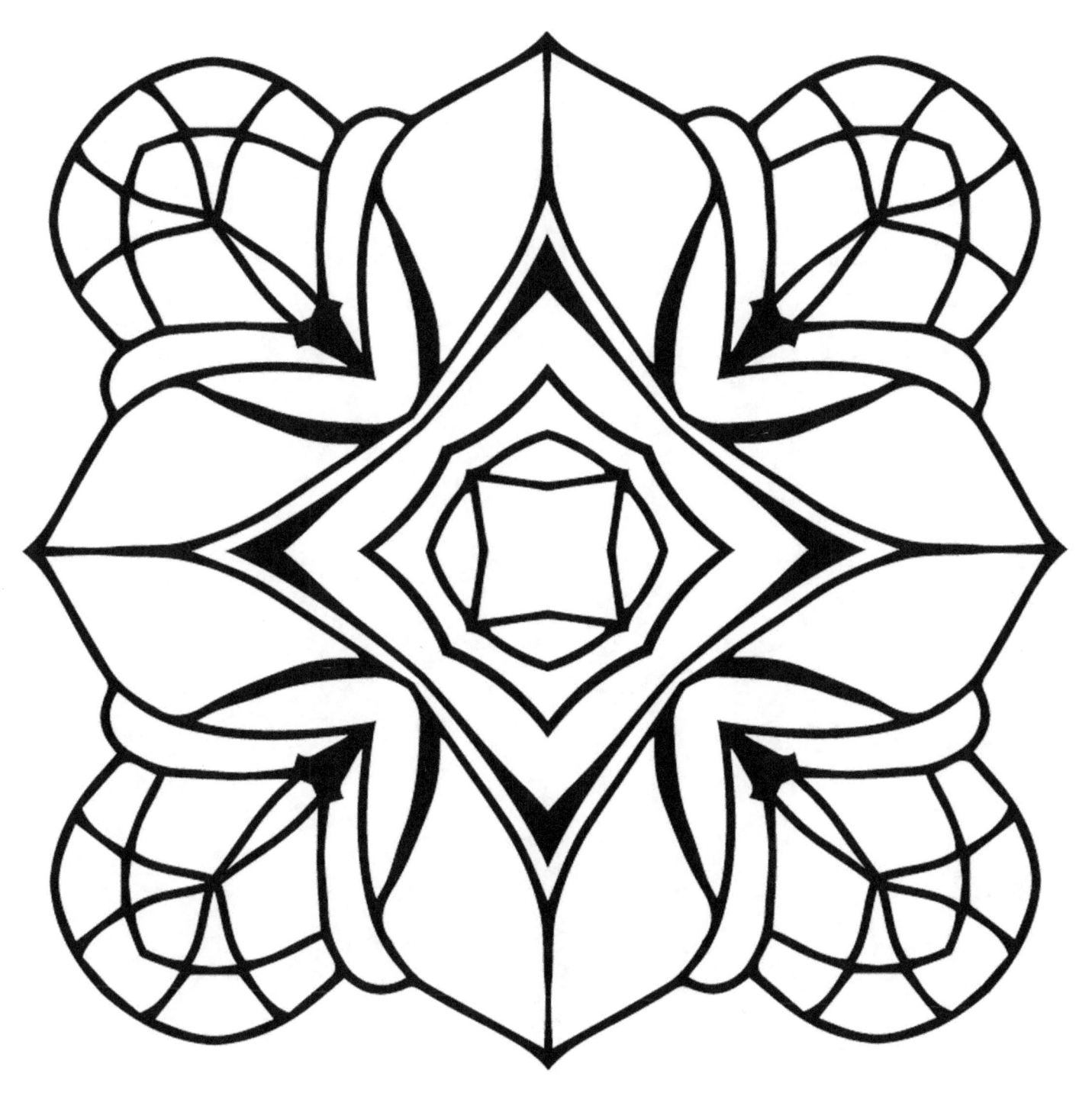

Kaleidoscopes Unleashed Beginner Volume One
Kelly Dombrowski

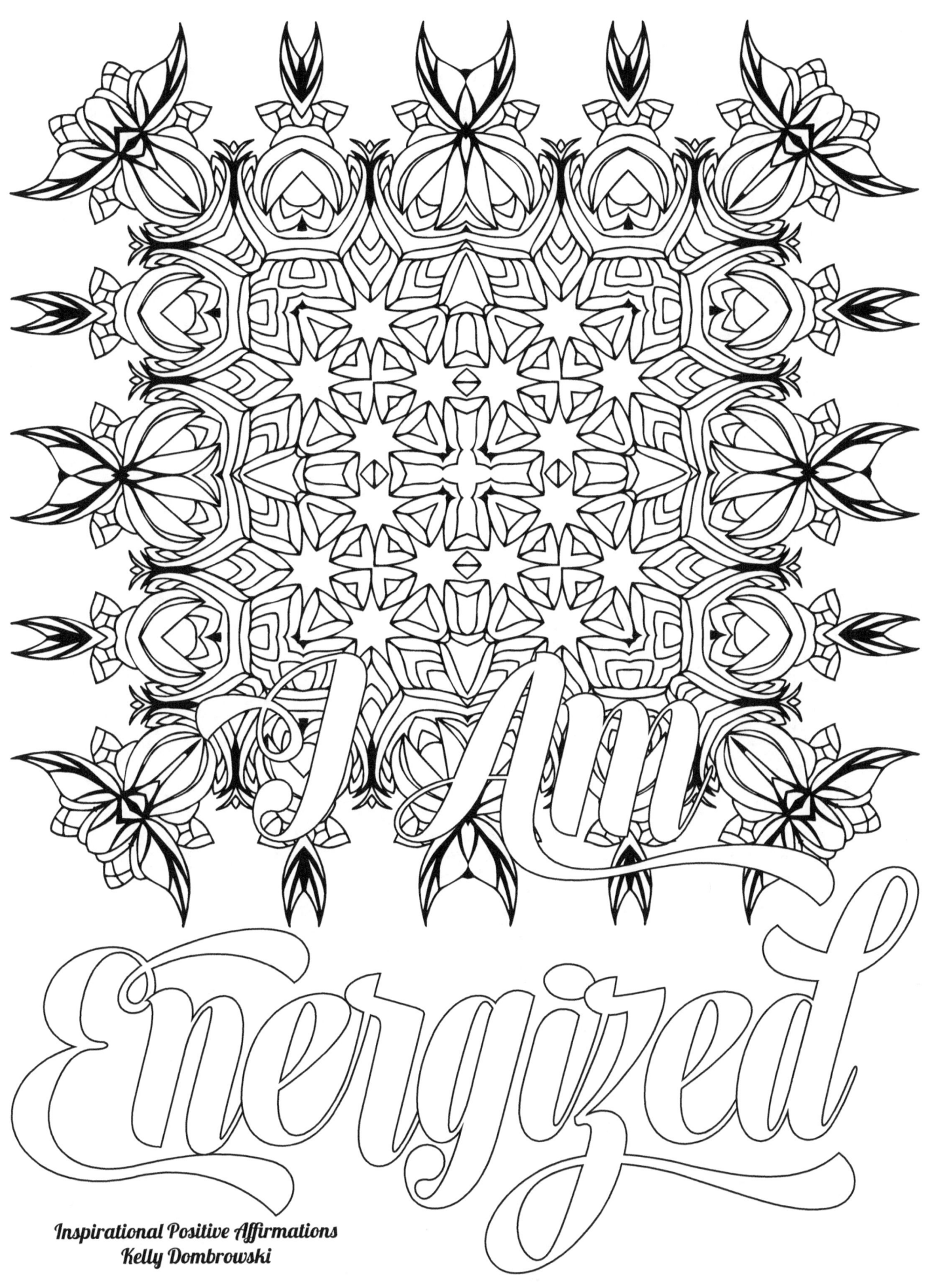

I Am Energized

Inspirational Positive Affirmations
Kelly Dombrowski

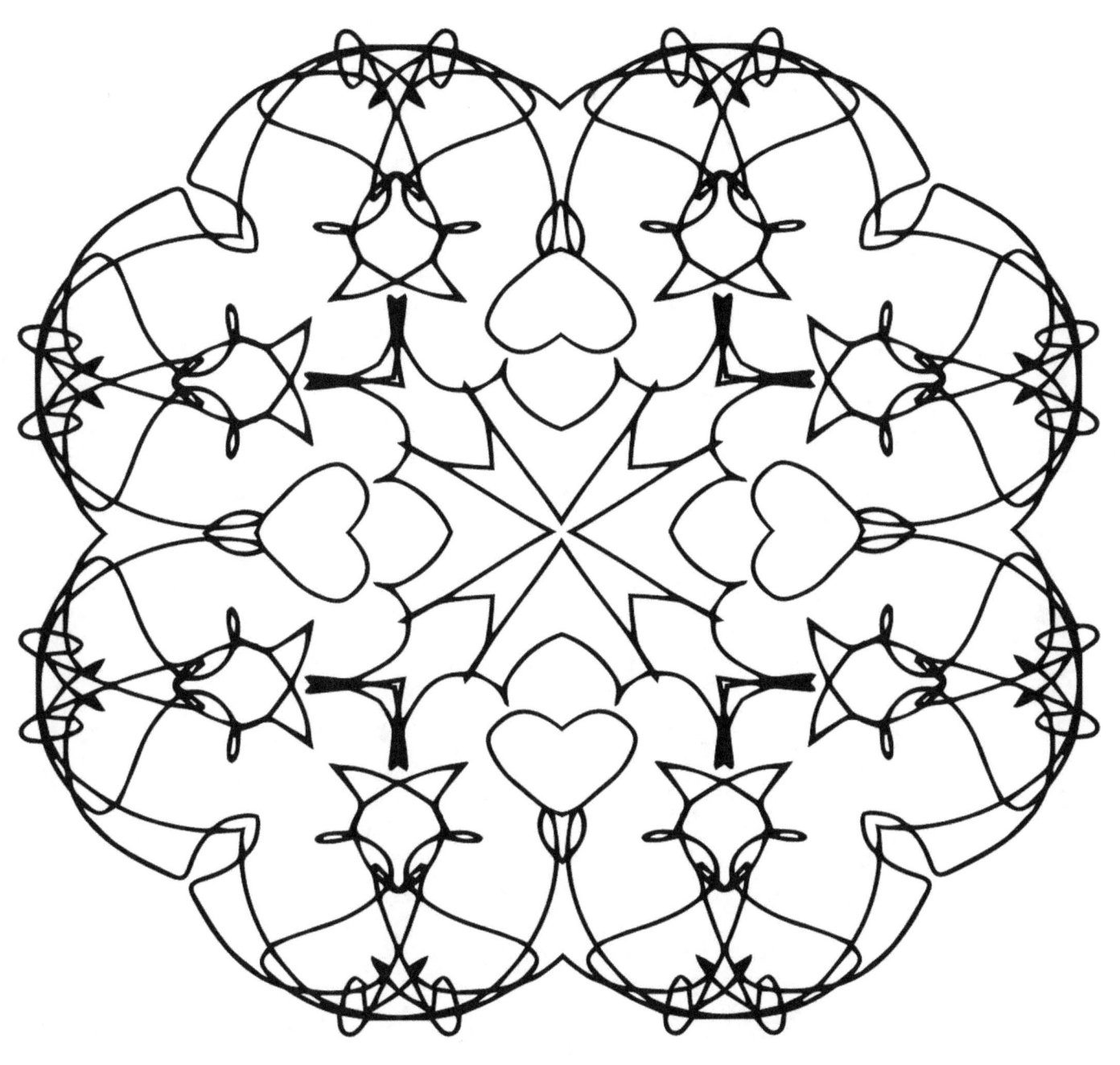

Sweet Curly Cue Designs Volume One
Kelly Dombrowski